G000154853

How to stitch for beginners

Basic instructional manual for making cross stitch with pictorial illustration

Charlotte Liam

Table of content

CHAPTER ONE

Basic instructions for creating cross stitch

Embroidery stitches in cross stitch are represented by tiny x's, and the job is done on a gridded cloth. By using a variety of colors, you may construct intricate sceneries or dainty patterns with the look and feel of needlework. If you're new to cross stitch, this guide will teach you the basics so you can get started right away.

Cross stitch is simple and straightforward for novices to

pick up and master since each cross stitch is made up of only two small stitches. This cross stitch beginner's guide has easy-to-follow instructions for a variety of beginner-friendly cross stitch patterns, as well as helpful hints for completing your first cross stitch project.

Let's examine the fundamentals of cross stitching for novices using the image in the next page. Because it can be done with any number of colors and doesn't need frequent rethreading of the needle, it's perfect for showcasing in a cross stitch beginner's guide. We are using 14-count Aida, the most widely available gridded fabric for cross stitch and an excellent option for those new to the craft. It is rigid and simple to manipulate, and the holes in the cloth are well delineated.

Chevron pattern Cross stitch
Charlotte Liam

When stitching on 14-count Aida, two strands of cotton are recommended. Embroidery cotton is sold in six-strand skeins; to thread the needle, separate the strands and then double them up.

Materials:

- Tapestry needle

- DMC stranded cotton

- 14-count aida fabric

Example one

Tip 1

First, tie the end of two lengths of cross stitch thread together and use them to thread one of your cross stitch needles. The knot is left on the surface of the fabric while the needle is inserted into the aida a little distance from the starting point.

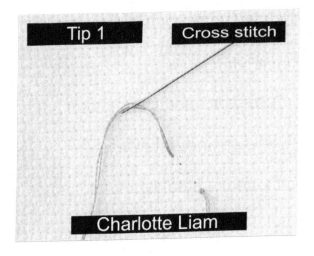

Tip 1   Cross stitch

Charlotte Liam

After the thread has been properly secured, we will snip this off. The waste knot technique refers to the practice of beginning a cross stitch project with a knot.

Tip 2

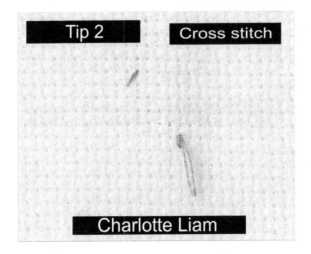

Tip 2   Cross stitch

Charlotte Liam

With the help of our free chevrons cross stitch design chart, stitch back toward your beginning knot. In this design, each dot corresponds to one cross stitch. Make a diagonal stitch for the initial section of the stitch. It should be placed over a single aida block with the long side facing up.

Tip 3

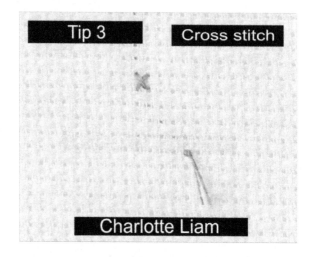

To finish the cross stitch, create a second diagonal stitch, this time from bottom right to top left, crossing over the first stitch you made. Colors on the chart correspond to stranded cotton, and you may use any combination of those colors to create this simple pattern.

Tip 4

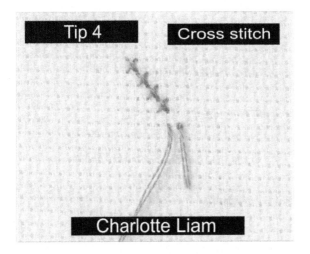

Carry on towards your beginning knot, being sure to tie your thread securely on the back. Cut the knot off when you get to it. To complete a thread, just slide it through the back of the stitches several times to secure it, and then trim the excess.

Example two

Equipments:

- Cross-stitch cloth

- Embroidery thread

- A needle and scissorsFirst

Tip 1: Start

Slipper the needle and cut a

short length of embroidery thread.

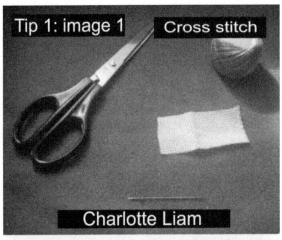

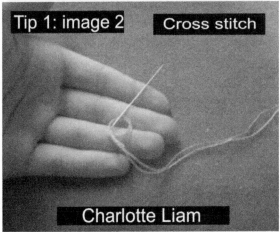

Tip 2: Single cross stitch

First, you'll need to take the embroidered cloth and insert the needle into one of the predrilled holes as shown in image 1. Next, insert the needle as indicated in Image 3, pull the thread to create a point, and insert the needle into the fourth hole as shown in the forth image .And a cross stitch has been started!

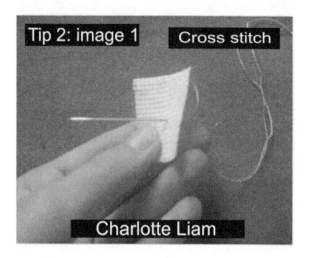

Tip 2: image 1   Cross stitch

Charlotte Liam

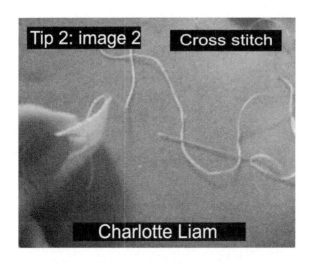

Tip 2: image 2 — Cross stitch — Charlotte Liam

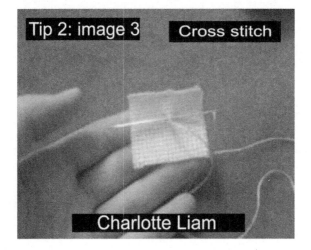

Tip 2: image 3 — Cross stitch — Charlotte Liam

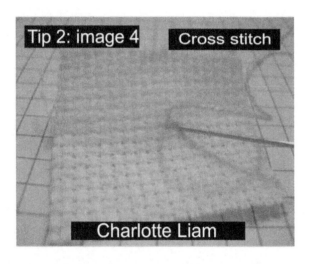

Tip 2: image 4 — Cross stitch — Charlotte Liam

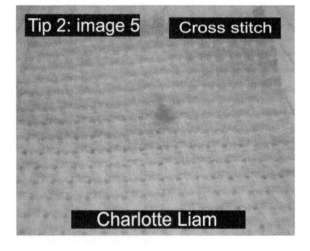

Tip 2: image 5 — Cross stitch — Charlotte Liam

Tip 3: Create a lot of cross stitched items

In this phase, we will do three cross stitches, however there are many more possible variations. Images 1 and 2 show how to start stitching by inserting the needle and leaving the tip on the wrong side of the fabric, images 3 and 4 show how many times to repeat this process to achieve the desired number of stitches, and finally images 5 and 6 show how to start stitching in reverse. It's finished!

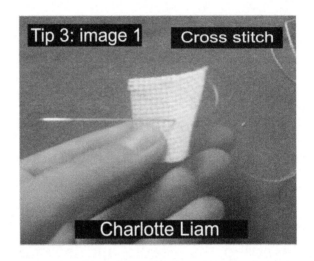

Tip 3: image 1 — Cross stitch

Charlotte Liam

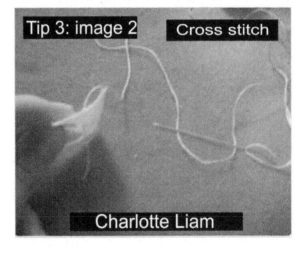

Tip 3: image 2 — Cross stitch

Charlotte Liam

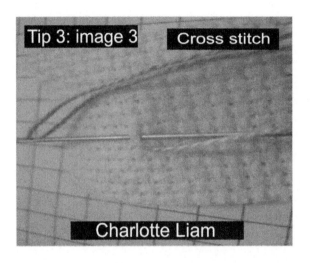

Tip 3: image 3 — Cross stitch — Charlotte Liam

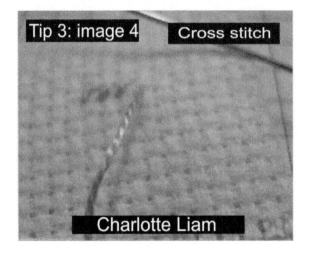

Tip 3: image 4 — Cross stitch — Charlotte Liam

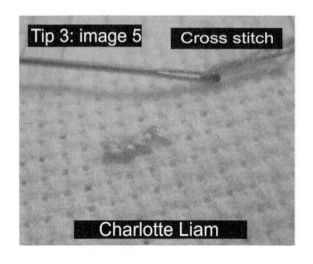

Tip 3: image 5   Cross stitch

Charlotte Liam

CHAPTER TWO

Different varieties of cross stitch

It's important you know some types of cross stitch in order for you to be able to handle some crucial cross stitching works. The following are some types of cross stitch you should know as a beginner.

1. Stitching using a herringbone pattern

The powerful Herringbone stitch is really just a fancy take on the standard cross stitch.

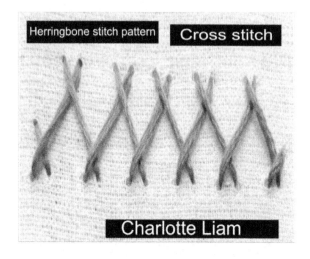

Herringbone stitch pattern · Cross stitch · Charlotte Liam

2. Stitching a cross across itself

The horizontal and vertical legs of a cross stitch are doubled for a double cross stitch. The cross stitches may be made quickly and easily, and then the vertical and horizontal stitches can be added on top. Smyrna cross stitch is another, fancier term for this pattern.

Stitching cross across itself — Cross stitch

Image 1

Charlotte Liam

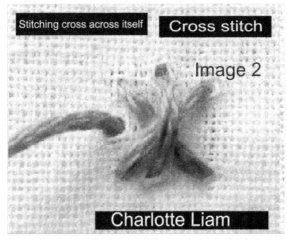

Stitching cross across itself — Cross stitch

Image 2

Charlotte Liam

3. Three-dimensional reverse cross stitch

One of the cross stitch's legs has been split in two for this design.

Three dimensional reverse cross stitch Cross stitch

Charlotte Liam

4. Lengthy cross stitch

This stitch has one leg that is longer than the other and is worked by beginning in the middle of the preceding cross stitch.

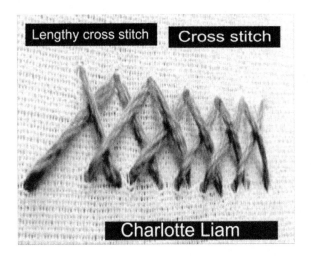

Lengthy cross stitch   Cross stitch

Charlotte Liam

5. Rice stitch

Starting with a row of cross stitches, this pattern incorporates a four-pointed star stitch into the empty squares, often using a contrasting thread color.

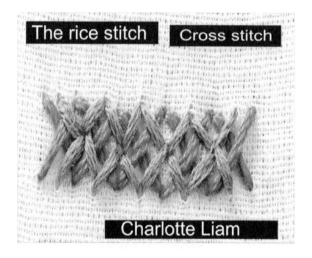

The rice stitch   Cross stitch

Charlotte Liam

6. Hungarian Cross-Stitch

The thread is put flat and a cross stitch is produced on top. Create a grid layout, as seen below, then fill it with upright cross stitch.

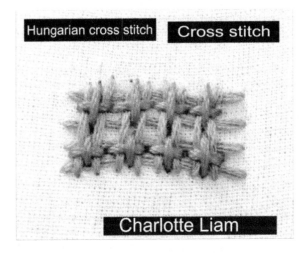

Hungarian cross stitch Cross stitch

Charlotte Liam

7. Cross Stitch, With Spaces

The cross stitches in this stitch are separated from one another. Make the half cross stitch first, then return to fill it, just as you would while doing the cross stitch in rows.

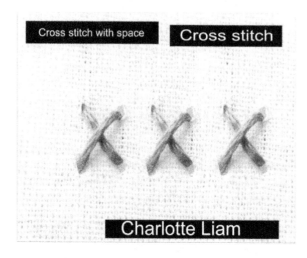

8. Italian X-Stitch

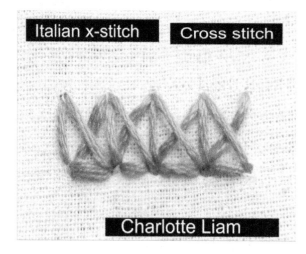

This is a sample of bordered cross stitch. Construction looks as the example image. When completed in a series of rows, this pattern resembles a box-work of cross stitches.

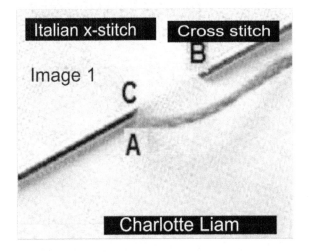

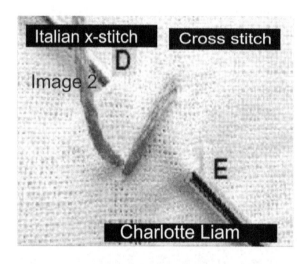

Italian x-stitch Cross stitch

Image 2

D

E

Charlotte Liam

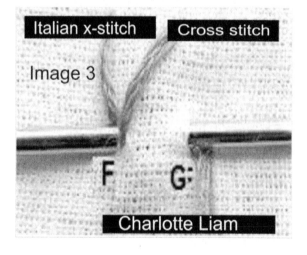

Italian x-stitch Cross stitch

Image 3

F G

Charlotte Liam

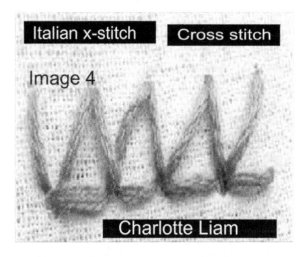

Image 4 — Italian x-stitch / Cross stitch — Charlotte Liam

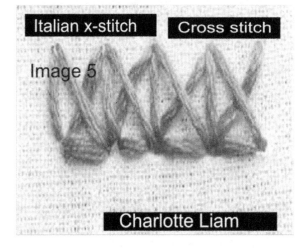

Image 5 — Italian x-stitch / Cross stitch — Charlotte Liam

9. Greek stitch

The central thread of this four-part vertical cross stitch crosses over itself to produce a knot.

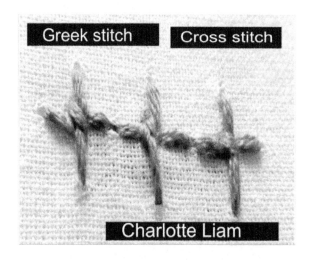

Greek stitch   Cross stitch

Charlotte Liam

10. Herringbone stitched twice

The basic herringbone row is expanded with an additional set of herringbone stitches in this

technique.   Typically,   a
contrasting color is used for this.

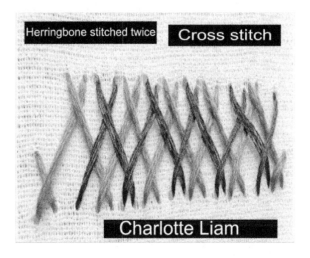
Herringbone stitched twice   Cross stitch
Charlotte Liam

There are standards that must
be met regardless of the method
of cross stitching used. In a
given section of a pattern, all
the cross stitches are the same
size. Therefore, the stitching has
to be uniform. That is, the
thread should be laid out

consistently (if you are going left to right for the row, do this for all rows, so that when you come back the thread will be laid in the same way) for an attractive finished cross stitch project.

CHAPTER THREE

Easy steps to complete cross-stitch work

Practicing a skill like cross stitch has been shown to improve mental health, lessen worry, and provide immense satisfaction.

In this last section, you'll learn three excellent strategies for enhancing the visual appeal of your completed product.

1. Finishing cross stitch with various backings

If you're working on a bigger project and would want to

transfer it to a board, you have a few options. Foam board has piqued my curiosity since it is inexpensive and simple to deal with. To replicate this, all you need is some sturdy masking tape, scissors, and pins.

Sticky board and some lightweight batting might be another option. A hot glue gun may be useful for securing the corners, but otherwise the method is the same. You can go through cheap glue sticks extremely fast, so if you do decide to buy one, it's usually worth investing a bit more.

In fact, if you already have a wooden tray or frame lying around, you can easily upcycle it and use it as the background for your cross stitch without spending a lot of money.

2. Cross stitch bookmarks

What better way to combine your love of needlework with

your passion for books than with a personalized bookmark? Here's a quick and easy method for transforming your cross-stitched design into a functional bookmark.

You'll need pinking shears, cardboard, a sewing machine or needle and thread, a piece of backing fabric the same size as your final bookmark, and a piece of interlining.

Create a cardboard pattern in the desired final bookmark size before proceeding. Cut out using pinking shears after tracing it onto the cross stitch, the interlining, and the backing fabric for your bookmark.

Place the interlining in the centre of the sandwich, and then use a running stitch to affix the layers together. Verify that the proper side of your backing fabric is showing.

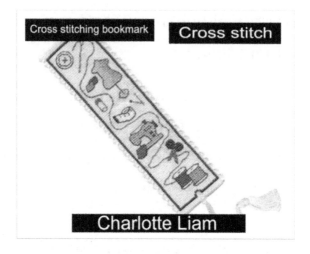

Cross stitching bookmark

Cross stitch

Charlotte Liam

3. How to end cross stitch work done in a hoop

Cross stitch done in a hoop may have its back neatly finished with a piece of felt. If you want to frame your completed cross stitch project, you'll need a piece of felt at least as large as the hoop, a needle, cotton thread, embroidery thread, a pencil, and the hoop you want to display it in.

Ending cross stitch in a hoop   Cross stitch

Charlotte Liam

To begin, trace the perimeter of your hoop onto the felt and then cut it out. When you're done, put your work back in the hoop and cut the fabric so that it's about an inch smaller all the way around. Start folding the fabric's raw edges in toward each other, right sides facing, using a needle and thread.

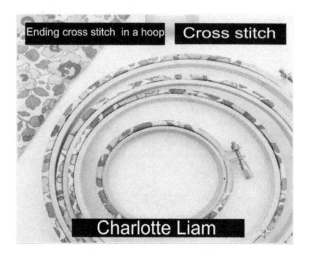

The finished cross stitch hoop will have a lattice pattern on the back to keep your cloth from shifting as you work. Finally, secure the felt to the cloth by sewing a blanket stitch around the circumference of the circle.

Ending cross stitch in a hoop

Cross stitch

Charlotte Liam

Felt may also be adhered with the use of glue, double-sided tape, or a hot glue gun. Fabric or decorative wooden back pieces may be purchased and attached to the hoop.

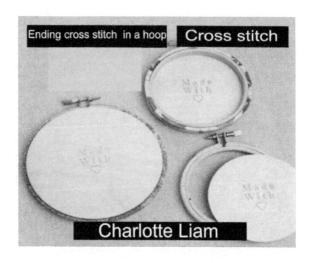

Ending cross stitch in a hoop

Cross stitch

Charlotte Liam

44

Printed in Great Britain
by Amazon

44720331R10030